Tip and Dip

Written by Catherine Baker

Collins

Kit	Tick
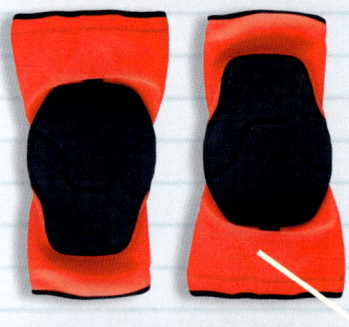	
 pads	

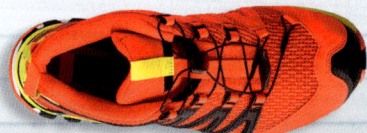	

Pick the kit.

Pop the kit in a pack.

pack

Sit at the top.

Dip and tip.

Nip in the gap.

the gap

Tip and dip in the pit.

pit

It can tip!

Dips, tips and kicks

13

Dip and tip

15

Review: After reading

Use your assessment from hearing the children read to choose any GPCs, words or tricky words that need additional practice.

Read 1: Decoding
- Turn to page 9 and ask the children to read the words **tip** and **dip**. Explain that the back wheel tips up and the front wheel dips down. Use the picture for support.
- Ask the children to read the following. Encourage them to point to the pair of letters that makes one sound. (/c/ "ck")

gap	can	kit	pick	kick

  o Ask: Can you blend in your head silently before reading these words aloud?

Read 2: Prosody
- Model reading **Kick it and tip!** on page 10, demonstrating an excited tone. Point to the exclamation mark and explain that this told you to read with extra feeling. Ask the children to have a go.
- Point to the exclamation mark on page 11. Ask: What feeling will you choose to read this? (e.g. *excitement, shock, surprise*) Model reading **It can tip!** and then ask the children to have a go.

Read 3: Comprehension
- Discuss any experiences the children have had of riding or watching bikes.
- Reread pages 8 and 9. Say: The people in this book are doing stunts, or special tricks, on BMX bikes. Discuss how BMX is different from riding a normal bike. Discuss how the stunts in this book can be dangerous. Children should not attempt these stunts themselves.
- Use the pictures on pages 14 and 15 to model how to recap the content of the book. Ask the children to describe the kit and the stunts, using vocabulary from the book. (e.g. **kick**, **dip**, **tip**)
- Bonus content: Look at the kit list on pages 2 and 3. Discuss the items shown (helmet, knee pads, elbow pads, trainers, gloves, water bottle, pump, BMX bike). Can the children explain what they are for?
- Bonus content: Turn to pages 12 and 13. Encourage the children to talk about the pictures and compare them. Ask: Which stunt do you think looks most impressive? Would you want to try any of them?